ANGRY YOUNG SNIGLETS

RICH HALL & FRIENDS
Illustrations by Arnie Ten

PAINTHEIST *(payn' the ist)*   n. One who never believes
a "wet paint" sign and must test it for himself.

ANGRY YOUNG SNIGLETS

(snig' lit):

any word that doesn't appear in the
dictionary, but should

Collier Books • Macmillan Publishing Company • New York
Collier Macmillan Publishers • London

Macmillan Publishing Company
866 Third Avenue, New York, N.Y. 10022
Collier Macmillan Canada, Inc.

Library of Congress Cataloging-in-Publication Data

Hall, Rich, 1954–
Angry young sniglets.

1. Words, New—English—Anecdotes, facetiae, satire, etc.   2. Vocabulary—
Anecdotes, facetiae, satire, etc.   I. Title.
PN6231.W64H29   1987   428.1′0207   87-10283
ISBN 0-02-012600-X

10   9   8   7   6   5   4   3   2   1

Designed by Antler & Baldwin, Inc.

PRINTED IN THE UNITED STATES OF AMERICA

To Barry Lippman,
with gratitude

CONTRIBUTORS

Joseph Baneth Allen Marc Anton Christy Barnshaw Michael Baron Silvia Blewett Thomas Boehne Sue Ann Bonhivert Tracy L. Calloway Marc Campbell Brad Cooper Rich Davison David, Lori and Karen Dow Dean Ehrman Keith Encapera Robert Faircloth Chip and Chris Feazel Gail Feddern Jerry Furst Joe Gardner Sher Bird Garfield Aron Goldman David, Thomas, and William Hahner **Rich Hall** Ed Hambrick Donald W. Harney Alan Hawes Dave Highben Neal Hirsch Michele G. Hudson Renee Julian Christopher, Katherine, Paula, and Tom Kiske Brian Korn Joel Krumerman Hugh Lawson III Megan MacCallum Becky Mack Jon Marcaccini Neil McNicholas Signe Moss Dan Nace   Mary Jo Nesspor Steve Novich Peter Ochs Brian O'Donnell Jean O'Sullivan Vincent Parry Pvt. Michael R. Porter Kristen Reed Billy Sanders E. Schimek Lynn Schumacher John C. Severance, Jr. David Sherman Rachel Sherman Siegfried Shyu Robert Spokane Rev. Andrew Steinman Rebecca Steinman Joel Sullivan G. Tammsaar Eric Torgerson Dick Vanhooser Richard M. Weatherly L. T. Williams W. A. Williamson Dave Witter

Jean O'Sullivan, assistant to Rich Hall and Pat Tourk Lee

CONTENTS

ADAM 69
(ad' um six tee nyn')

n. Two cop cars parked in opposite directions exchanging information.

AEROBICROACHER
(ayr oh' bi kroch ur)

n. A person who gradually gravitates toward another's space while exercising.

AIR LASER
(ayr' lay zur)

n. The stream of high-velocity air above your airplane seat that can be adjusted to: (a) sting your face, (b) sting your ear, (c) sting your hair.

AIRPLAUSE
(ayr plawz')

n. Gratuitous ovation awarded a pilot on completion of a safe landing.

ALPOGOALIE
(al po go' lee)

n. Any dog smart enough to use its paw to pin down a dog dish.

ALTIPULP
(al' tih pulp)

n. The few remaining magazines (*Poultry Digest, Ultra Triathlete*, etc.) you come across when you go to the rack for reading material while in flight.

AMAZINGRAZIN
(uh may' zin gray zin)

n. The ability to cut a piece of cake with a little plastic fork on a flimsy paper plate while holding a big drink, a cute little napkin, and a cup of nuts.

ARROWNEOUS
(ayr ow' nee us)

adj. The quality of one who drives against the arrow in a parking lot.

ASPITRON
(ah' spit ron)

n. The tiny brain in an aspirin that tells it *exactly* what part of the afflicted body to go to.

AUDIOSIS
(odd ee oh' sis)

v. Hearing a sound you don't notice until it stops, e.g., the furnace or refrigerator shutting off.

BABYBUFFERS
(bay' bee buf furz)

n. People who hang "Baby on Board" signs in their car windows, as if the rest of us are driving around thinking, "You know, I'd *like* to plow into that car, but I don't want to hurt the baby."

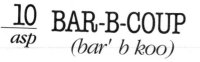

BAR-B-COUP
(bar' b koo)

n. When your uncle or any other obnoxious relative commandeers the outdoor barbecue grill against your wishes.

BEDWINDS
(bed' windz)

n. Those mysterious drafts that always prevent a sheet from drifting perfectly onto the mattress.

BIBBLAGE
(bib' lij)

n. The angle of one's body while scanning the library shelf.

BICOMA
(bib kom' uh)

n. The nonfunctioning pen you return to the pen caddy, thinking *somehow* it will come back to life at a later date.

BILBOUS
(bil' buhs)

n. The one person on every trip compelled to read every passing billboard aloud.

BINGOBABBLE
(bing' go bab bul)

n. The increase of vocal activity that occurs when dozens of people are only one number away from reaching *Bingo*.

BLIX
(blikz)

n. The moving part on the inside of an ice cream scooper that carves and ejects a single scoop.

BLOBIAGE
(blo' be ij)

n. The propaganda sticker on hand-driers that attempts to convince you they're preferable to paper towels.

BOMB BIN
(bom' bin)

n. The plastic tub at airport security counters where you deposit small metal objects before passing through. (NOTE: HEY KIDS! DON'T USE THIS WORD AT THE AIRPORT!)

BOWFFANT
(bau font')

v. The pastime of turning your dog's ears inside out and folding them across his head, even though the dog seldom appreciates the levity of the situation.

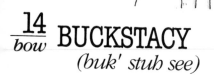

BUCKSTACY
(buk' stuh see)

n. The joy of finding money you forgot you had in your coat pocket.

BULLSHIDARTIST
(bul' shih dart ist)

n. Person who positions his darts directly into the bull's-eye at the end of a game so the next person entering the room will think he's a dart wizard.

BULLSLOTS
(bul' slotz)

n. Post office mail slots marked "In Town," "Out of Town," etc., which everyone knows empty into the same bin.

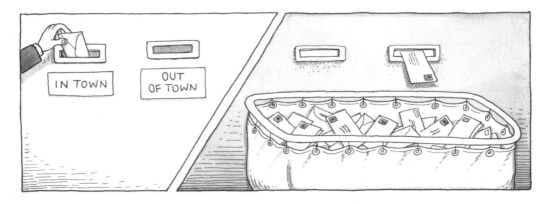

BUTTBLOTTING FLUID
(but' blot ing flu' id)

n. The mysterious blue stuff they pour onto diapers in diaper commercials to demonstrate their absorbency.

BUYZANTINE
(by' zan teen)

adj. An architectural style (prevalent in museums) designed so visitors can exit only via the gift shop.

CANAFLATIONARY ZONE
(kan uh flay' shun ayr ee zon)

n. The area on a book or magazine that makes you glad you're an American.

U.S.
$2.95

CAN.
$3.95

CARSNIGLEGENS
(kar snig' luh jenz)

n. Things that cause cancer that scientists haven't discovered yet.

CARTIPILLAR
(kar' tih pi lur)

n. A line of cars waiting to get on the freeway at rush hour.

CHARCOPHILE
(char' ko fyl)

n. A person who loves burnt food.

CHERK
(churk)

n. The person in the grocery line who writes a check for three items.

CHUFF
(chuhf)

n. The line of grease you always find on your right trouser leg when dismounting a bicycle.

CINEMUTATION
(sin uh mew tay' shun)

n. The drastic change in the story line when a book is made into a movie.

CINESLOUCH
(sih' nuh slowch)

n. The position one adopts preparatory to a shock scene in a horror movie.

CINETRAP
(sin' uh trap)

n. The inability to leave the movie theater because your date insists on watching the credits.

CLINGUINI
(kling gwee' nee)

n. That one strand of pasta that remains stuck to the bottom of the pan as you're emptying it into the colander.

COASTERNETS
(ko stur netz')

n. The ratchety sound you hear on a roller coaster seconds before it crests and hysteria ensues.

CORPUS NEGLECTI
(kor pus nuh glek' ty)

n. The transformation of a former high-school athlete into a beer-bellied, middle-aged man.

COVERLICIOUS
(kuh vur lish' us)

n. The warm feeling of waking up on a cold morning and discovering you have another 20 minutes to sleep.

CRETINGER
(kret' in jer)

n. The toll-free number printed on credit cards that you are instructed to call when your credit card has been lost.

CRIMPLAP
(krim' plap)

n. The short stroll taken when trying on a new pair of shoes, before deciding whether to buy them or not.

CRIPPLECREEPS
(krip' ul kreeps)

n. People who insist on trying out your crutches when you are injured.

CROOKLIGHT
(kruk' lyt)

n. The one light you always leave on to discourage burglars.

CRUMBDUNDANCY
(krum dun' dan see)

n. The act of revacuuming parts of your car for no reason other than to use up the remaining time on the coin-operated vacuum machine.

CUBBAGE
(kuh' bij)

n. The ivy that covers the walls at Wrigley Field.

DEFRECIATE
(deh fre' she ayt)

v. While driving home from a fast-food restaurant, stealing an equal amount of fries from each bag so the recipients will think they just got small portions.

DE JAVA
(day zha va')

n. The feeling, as you put sugar in your coffee, that you've already put sugar in your coffee.

DELTA VISTA
(del' tuh vis' tuh)

n. The principle that states on any flight the "spectacular view" the pilot is describing is through the opposite window.

DESTINESIA
(des tin ee' zha)

n. The act of entering a room and forgetting why.

DIRTWAFFLES
(dir' twah fulz)

n. Incriminating bits of preformed dirt that fall off the bottoms of tennis shoes onto clean floors.

DISASTASTACK
(diz as' ta stak)

n. Any precariously balanced pyramid of cans or bottles blocking a grocery aisle.

DONETICS
(do net' iks)

n. Any attempt to communicate with the donut waitress on the other side of the case.

DREAMONIUM
(dree mon' ee um)

n. The metallic coating on a lottery ticket that separates you from a million bucks a year for life.

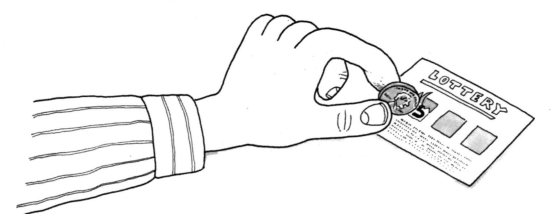

DRIVERIE
(dry' vur ee)

n. Any daydream experienced while driving that causes you to miss your turn.

DUDNOBS
(dud' nobz)

n. The fake drawers beneath the sink that everyone tries to pull open.

EFAMATE
(ef' uh mayt)

v. To eliminate a dangerous automobile noise by turning up the volume on the radio.

ELEVENCE
(el' uh vins)

n. The silence that pervades a crowded elevator when the doors close.

EMENEMINIZE
(em 'n em' en ize)

v. Consuming one's M&M's by color groups.

EUFRAIN
(yu frayn')

n. The amount of time (usually four words into the song) it takes a group of people singing "Happy Birthday" to reach a common key.

EXAMINISCIENCE
(eg zam' in ih sy enz)

n. The ability of the computer or testing official to *somehow know* if you've used *anything but* a number two pencil.

FACINE
(fay seen')

n. The amount of Visine or Murine you dribble on your cheek, up your nose, etc., before you finally get it in your eye.

FANIACS
(fan' ee aks)

n. People in the crowd at a sporting event who have painted their faces in their team colors.

FATFINETUNER
(fat' fyn toon' ur)

n. The knob at the top of the bathroom scale.

FLOUND
(flownd)

v. To use one's free arm for balance when lugging a heavy gas can or suitcase.

GATE 99

FLUTCH
(flutch)

n. The jerk one's body makes when one thinks one has lost his/her wallet.

FOODGITIVES
(food' juh tivz)

n. The individual vegetables (or tater tots) in a TV dinner tray that escape over the wall into the Salisbury Steak Zone.

FORKORRAL
(for' kor al)

n. The plastic tray used to organize and separate silverware.

FRANCIS SCOTT KEYS
(fran' sis skaht keez')

n. The notes of the "Star-Spangled Banner" that only trained opera singers are able to reach.

FRINGE RELATIVE
(frinj rel' uh tiv)

n. Any relative who appears in a smaller photo stuck into the corner of the frame (i.e., a relative not important enough to appear in his/her own frame).

F-SHOCK
(ef' shok)

n. The discovery, after having a flash photo taken of yourself, that you are albino.

FURNACULARS
(fur nac' u lurz)

n. The nocturnal sounds made by furnaces that convince you burglars are downstairs.

FUZZBUZZ
(fuz' buz)

n. The overwhelming urge that forces otherwise sensible people to "thank" police officers for traffic tickets.

GESUNDTIME
(guh zoon' tym)

n. That agonizing moment between the detection of an imminent sneeze and its actual execution.

GHOSTSCREENING
(gost' skreen ing)

v. Pretending that you are not the person the caller wants to speak to so that you can screen your calls.

GIBLUMP
(gib' lump)

n. The foil-wrapped turkey that sits in the refrigerator for days after Thanksgiving.

GIMMIENNIUM
(gih mee' in ee um)

n. The amount of time one lets pass when attempting to be the "eighth lucky caller," "third lucky caller," etc.

GLEEDEBRIS
(glee' de bree)

n. The pile of wrapping paper and ribbon left after all the gifts have been opened.

GLOOB
(gloob)

n. Air bag created in the front of one's trunks when entering a swimming pool.

GLOOPIUM
(glu' pee um)

n. The area at the bottom of the sundae glass the spoon can't quite reach.

GLOVOCITY
(glub vos' it ee)

n. When chasing a baseball, the increase of speed achieved by throwing off one's mitt.

GLUBBULE
(glub' yule)

n. The eerie announcement, appearance, and ascension of the bubble in a water cooler.

GOOFYTTI
(goo fee' tee)

n. The scribblings on the walls at Disneyland.

GOBBLEMENTS
(gob' luh ments)

n. The decorative miniature chef hats placed on the ends of turkey drumsticks.

GROCESSES
(grow' ses iz)

n. The wasted area of space on a shelf caused by round cans meeting at their circumferences.

GUFFAWNIX
(guh fahw' nix)

n. Uproarious laughter which must be forcibly squelched due to its being inappropriate at the time, e.g., in the classroom, at a business meeting.

HAMNESIA
(ham nee' zhuh)

n. A gap in your memory that allows you to forget your diet and pig out on goodies.

HANNAH-OBSCURA
(hah' nuh ohb skur' uh)

n. The unintelligible line in the Flintstone theme song (". . . through the courtesy of Fred's big feet").

HASBROGANY
(haz brog' uh nee)

n. The crime of allowing a child who does not meet the "age and up" requirement to participate in a board game.

HELICRATE
(hel' ih krate)

n. Any mobile home in a tornado-prone area. (See also **MOBICIDE**.)

HICCUMUMBO
(hik uh mum' bo)

n. The preposterous rituals that sensible, God-believing people will resort to to get rid of hiccups (salt-tossing, cemetery visitations, incantations, etc.).

HOLEYMOLEY
(ho lee mow' lee)

n. That tiny hole in your pocket that inevitably grows on a diet of coins and keys.

HOORDER
(huor' dur)

n. A delaying tactic used by waiters/waitresses of placing your check facedown on the table. (So-called because this gives them time to escape before you turn it over and start screaming, "Hoorder's this!?)

H$_2$OT
(aych tu aht')

n. The hot water that comes out of a hose after it has sat in the sun all day.

HOUSE CHANGE
(haus' chanj)

n. The twelve cents that can always be found under the couch cushion.

HOWUZITIZE
(hau wuz' it ize)

v. To scan the faces of exiting moviegoers in an attempt to determine the quality of the film.

HUMOMENTUM
(hu mo men' tum)

n. Precious extra feet gained in an out-of-gas car by thrusting one's body forward.

HYPOCRITULATION
(hip oh krit yew lay' shun)

n. The seemingly joyous reaction of the runners-up as they surround the winner at a beauty pageant.

INADEQUILL
(in ad' uh kwil)

n. The feeling one gets when not answering a letter promptly.

INDYSECOND
(in' dee sek und)

n. The moment of hesitation you have just before gunning your car and running the yellow light.

INVISIVOIDANCE
(in viz uh voy' dans)

n. The ability to disappear in order to avoid saying hello to someone.

JACKSTOP
(jak' stop)

n. The stop you make fifteen feet from the pickup window to make sure your order is all there and to make adjustments (straw through drink, etc.) for eating and driving at the same time.

KATPRANO
(kat prah' no)

n. The high voice one uses when summoning a cat.

KIDFUSION
(kid few' zhun)

n. The state wherein a parent stumbles over the names of all her children before calling the right one, i.e., "Matt, Ruth, Ken, George, *BOB*, get over here!"

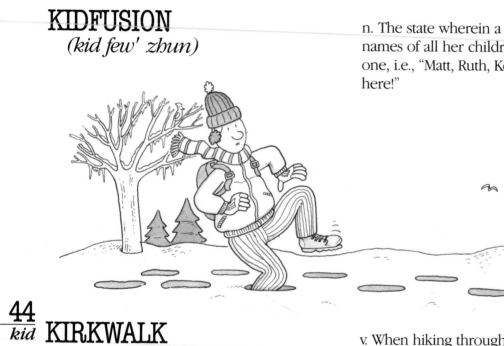

KIRKWALK
(kir' kwok)

v. When hiking through snow, using the footsteps of one who has boldly gone before you.

KLEPTORCEPTORS
(klep' tor sep torz)

n. The two-foot-long (security overkill) plastic device encasing cassette tapes at record stores.

KNUCKLECHEESE
(nuk' l cheez)

n. Shreds of skin lost when grating cheese.

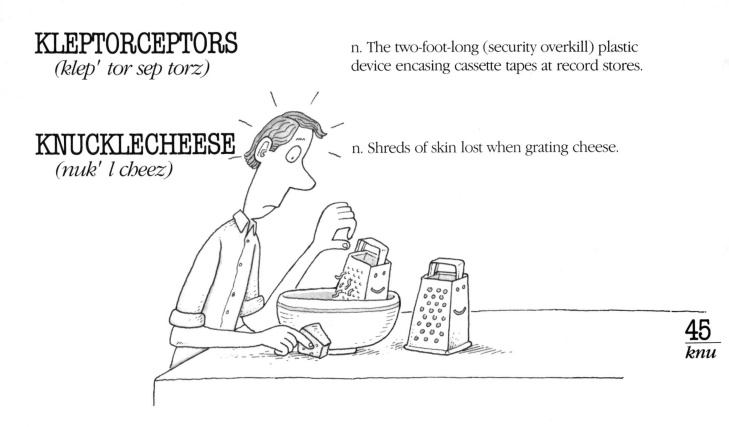

LACTO-OSTEOKIBBLETIC
(lak' tow os' tee oh kih bleh' tik)

adj. The secret urge to taste Milk-Bones or dry dog food just to get an idea of what your dog has to look forward to for the rest of his life.

LACTOSPANSION
(lak tow span' shun)

n. Phenomenon that occurs when a cup of milk drops to the floor, producing enough milk to fill three cups.

LARF
(larf)

v. To lick and retain a fork for dessert.

LAVA-JAVA
(lah' vuh jah vuh)

n. The filled-to-the-rim cup of coffee at fast-food drive-ins that is usually 4000 degrees Fahrenheit.

LOCKOBLANKO
(lok' oh blan' ko)

n. Trauma of returning to school from Christmas vacation and being unable to remember one's locker combination.

LOISANBOBS
(low' ihs an bohbz)

n. Christmas card signed in first names only (giving you absolutely no idea who these people are).

LOONIEBABBLING
(loo' nee bab ling)

v. The act of inhaling the contents of a helium-filled balloon and talking like Alvin and the Chipmunks.

LOOTCHUTE
(loot' shoot)

n. The vacuum tube used in drive-through banks to move money back and forth to customers.

LUMILUMP
(loo' mih lump)

n. The stackup of moviegoers at the top of the aisle waiting for a light scene to appear on the screen so they can see the seats.

MALLWALTZIST
(mahl walt' zist)

n. Person hired to demonstrate organs and pianos in shopping malls.

MAJURY
(mah' ju ree)

n. Blatant lies and illogic that mothers use to discourage "dangerous" activity among children (i.e., "What if your face freezes like that?").

MARMAL
(mar' mul)

n. The bits of orange peel suspended in marmalade.

MATTRIHISS
(mat' rih his)

n. The tiny amount of air that always escapes before sealing off an air mattress.

MAWLK
(mawlk)

n. The one deflated or "factory irregular" malted milk ball in every box.

McMAGNAMAT
(mik mag' nuh mat)

n. The paper place mat on the McDonald's tray that adheres, no matter how much you try to shake it into the trash receptacle.

MELON-DIXON LINE
(mel' un dix' un lyn)

n. The point of the watermelon you do not eat below because someone told you it would give you a stomachache.

MENUGE
(men' u zhe)

n. The person among a tableful of diners silently elected to hand all the menus back to the waitress.

MERTON EFFECT
(mur' tun ef fekt')

n. Theory that if you are in a fast-moving elevator and you jump up, you will never touch the floor again.

MOBICIDE
(mo' bih syd)

n. The stupefying principle that states the most tornado-prone areas attract the highest number of mobile homes. (See also **HELICRATE**.)

MODOWN
(mow' down)

n. The final phase of lawn cutting. The point at which one stops mowing in an up and down pattern and starts mowing in an angular pattern.

MOMETER
(ma' me tur)

n. The back part of a mom's hand that, when placed to a child's forehead, "knows" if the kid is running a fever or not.

MONOPUTZ
(ma' no putz)

n. The one person in every Monopoly game who feels compelled to say, "Wouldn't it be great if this money were real?"

MOOL
(mool)

n. The little container on the side of a cash register where your change appears.

MR. CEMENTEE
(mis' tur see men' tee)

n. Any cement truck with colorful dots painted on it, presumably to attract children.

MUNCHBUNCH
(munch' bunch)

n. The huddle that forms around the cake and cookies at an office celebration.

NABISCITES
(neh bih' skyts)

n. Deteriorated cookie particles in the milk.

NACLICAL JOKE
(nak' lik ul jok)

n. Gleeful practice of loosening salt shaker caps, even though you know you won't be around to savor the outcome.

NAD
(nad)

n. 18.4 cm. The distance from a driver's out-stretched fingertips to a ticket dispenser in a parking lot.

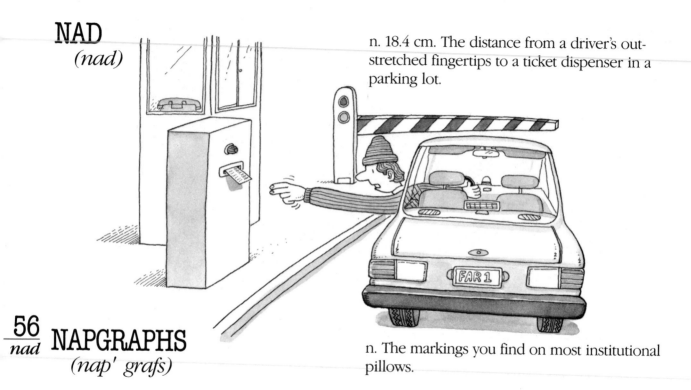

NAPGRAPHS
(nap' grafs)

n. The markings you find on most institutional pillows.

NASALSTALGIA
(nay zul stahl' juh)

n. Special smells that bring you back to another place and time, e g., your mother's kitchen.

NEBULANTS
(neh' bu lantz)

n. Those product ingredients that follow the phrase, "contains one or more of the following," as if the manufacturers themselves don't know what goes in the stuff.

NEWSPAMPER
(nooz' pam pur)

n. The plastic bag that appears on your newspaper on days when it rains or snows.

NOGGENAVIGATION
(nog uh nav uh gay' shun)

n. The ability of parents to guide their small children around by the tops of their heads.

NOMOR
(no' mor)

n. The red slash and circle that is the symbol of Universal Hatred.

NOODLIUM
(nood' lee um)

n. The tiny window through which you are allowed to view spaghetti and pasta.

NORTONISMS
(nor' tun iz umz)

n. "Loosening up" motions made with the wrist before writing.

ODDIOVIDEO
(ah' dee oh vid' ee oh)

n. Inexplicable phenomenon of tuning into a TV show you've seen just once only to have it be a repeat of the exact same show.

ODGET
(ahd' jit)

n. Those extremely obscure crayons that will never be used because *nothing* in the universe is the color of cerise.

OOB
(oob)

n. The hollow tube left behind when the onion accidentally slithers out of the onion ring.

OPHEAD
(op' hed)

v. To smash one's head against the crease of a newspaper to get it to fold.

ORDACITY
(or das' ih tee)

n. The crafty way advertisers have of wording order forms ("Gentlemen, please send me . . . ," "Enclosed please find my check for . . . ," "I understand that if I am not fully satisfied . . .") so that it looks like we wrote them ourselves.

PAKILAPSE
(pak' uh laps)

n. The delay you have to endure at the 7-Eleven counter while the clerk walks over and extracts another roll of pennies from the MONEY FORT.

PAMPERY
(pam' pur ee)

n. The pretense of going through someone's stack of baby pictures slowly, making cooing sounds, etc., when you really want to flip through them like a deck of cards.

PARD
(pard)

n. The stubby, eraserless thing miniature golf courses and bowling alleys issue you, presumably to keep you from changing your score.

PAYALATOR
(pa yuh lay' tor)

n. The greasy plastic board service station attendants lend you when signing a credit card.

PEPSUNAMI
(pep su nam' ee)

n. When pouring a soft drink onto ice, the tidal wave of carbonation that cascades over the edge of the soft drink glass.

PETRIDENT
(peh' tri dent)

n. Old sticks of gum at the bottom of a woman's purse.

PETROULETTE
(pet ru let')

n. Risky game of driving with your fuel gauge below empty.

PEXZOOT
(pek zoot')

n. The small piece of lid that the electric can opener always passes over.

PIEBREAKERS
(py' bray kurz)

n. The "waves" on the top of a meringue pie.

PIELIGNMENT
(py lyn' ment)

n. When eating pie, arranging it so the pointed end is in line with one's chest.

POMOMADE
(pa' mom ayd)

n. Emergency grooming product (active ingredient: saliva) used by mothers to smooth kids' hair.

PONUNDRUMS
(po nun' drumz)

n. Those strange green mailboxes that are completely sealed off, the insides of which no civilian has ever witnessed.

PREMODEMOLITIONITION
(pre' mo deh mo lih' shun ih shun)

n. When the car ahead of you pulls too far out into the intersection, backs up, and you know that they have not put the car back into forward gear and will probably very shortly plow into you.

PUSHOPATHIC
(puh' sho path' ik)

adj. Having a secret urge to expedite the person ahead of you through a revolving door.

RADIOPORKTIVITY
(ray' dee oh pork tiv' uh tee)

n. The rainbows that form in two-week-old packaged meats.

ReMcAns
(re mik anz')

n. A pair of shoes with no wadding in the toes, leading you to believe they've been returned.

RESIDUDES
(rez' ih doodz)

n. Those old men you always see sitting around the lobbies of cheap hotels.

RINTINABULATION
(rin tin ab yew lay' shun)

n. The jingle of your dog's I.D. tags.

RORT
(rort)

n. The item in the copier left behind by the previous user which you sometimes also copy (thinking sooner or later the information could come in handy).

ROTISSERATE

(row tis' sur ayt)

v. The action of turning over to even out one's tan.

ROVERGENCE
(row vur' jens)

n. The endearing quality of wet dogs to get as close to you as possible before shaking themselves dry.

SACRIJIGGLE
(sak rih jig' gul)

v. Rustling the church offering plate without actually contributing.

SANIRISE
(sah' nih ryz)

n. The uncanny and embarrassing property of feminine products to defy gravity and float to the top of a woman's purse, making itself plainly visible to all upon opening.

SCANNICPANIC
(skan' ik pan' ik)

n. The act of tearing apart a living room in search of the television remote control instead of just walking over and *manually* turning on the TV.

SCANOOT
(skah noot')

n. The quick scan and removal of embarrassing items (photos, empty Häagen-Dazs containers, *People* magazine, etc.) when cleaning off the car seat for a passenger.

SEALYWHEELIE
(see' lee wee lee)

n. The startled reaction when you turn over in bed and realize there's no more bed in that direction.

SHIELDSNUGGLING
(sheeld' snug ling)

n. A widely held childhood belief (often carried into adulthood) that by pulling all bedcovers as closely around the body as possible, one will be immune from ghosts, goblins, burglars, etc.

SHURP
(shurp)

v. Holding your own breath when a character on the screen submerges himself in water.

SHWEE
(shwee)

n. The sound made by a door opening on "Star Trek."

SLEEVDINI
(Sleev dee' nee)

n. A person who fights his way out of a shirt without first unbuttoning the cuffs.

SLOLO
(slow' low)

n. A stranded penny in a five-cent gumball slot.

SNACKFRICTION
(snak frik' shun)

n. The act of jiggling popcorn or M&M's in your hand before popping them into your mouth, as if somehow this will "excite" them into tasting better.

SNACKTIVITY
(snak tiv' ih tee)

n. Any amusing table pastime (i.e., putting olives on the ends of one's fingers, "biting faces" into a slice of bread, etc.).

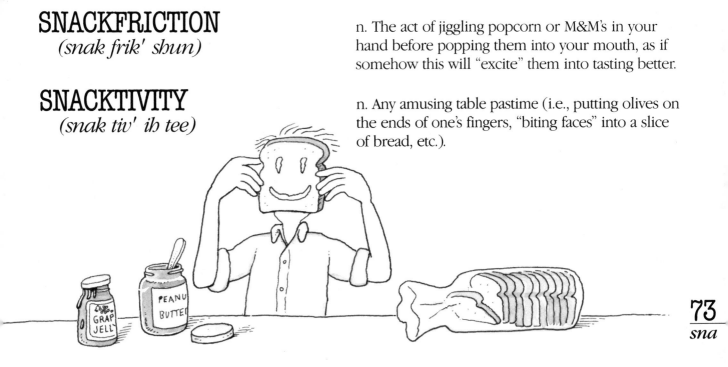

SNACTIONALS
(snak' shun ulz)

n. The crumbled cookies at the bottom of the package eaten without guilt since only *whole* cookies contain calories.

SNATWHAP
(snat' hwap)

v. To change a bed partner's snoring pattern with a knee-to-kidney thrust.

SNOCKER
(snok' ur)

n. The coin that wedges itself sideways in a coin tube and backs everything up.

SNOWLARPLEXUS
(snow lur plek' sus)

n. The part of the abdomen that sustains injury when you're shoveling snow and suddenly hit a rise in the sidewalk.

SOAP CANAVERAL
(sop' ka nav' ar ul)

n. The plastic wand that launches soap bubbles.

SONGLONGER
(song' long gur)

n. A person who always sings ". . . and many mooore" at the end of the "Happy Birthday" song.

SPALDRAWLS
(spal' drahlz)

n. Etched autographs in sports equipment that the manufacturers would like you to believe were personally carved by the athletes themselves.

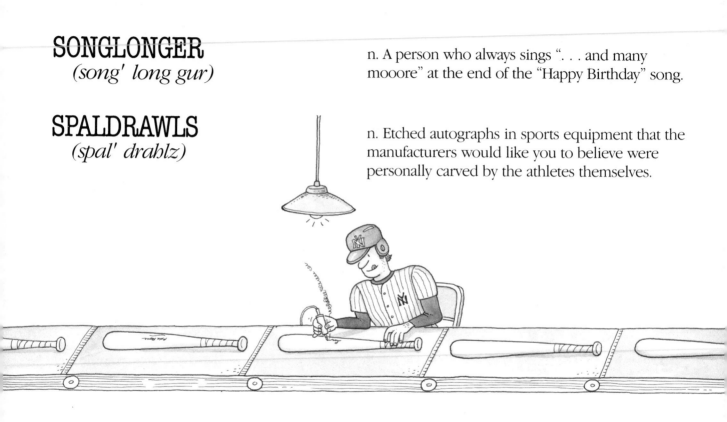

SPLATFALLEN
(splat' fal len)

n. The secret disappointment of reaching the end of a traffic jam and not seeing blood, gore, overturned vehicles, scattered currency, or anything spectacular enough to justify the delay.

SPUDPUDDLE
(spud pud' dul)

n. The area cleared out beside a stack of fries for catsup.

SQUADDLE
(skwah' dul)

n. The stooped-over position that an airplane window seat passenger endures while waiting for the other passengers to disembark.

SQUAKEZE
(skwahk eez')

n. The language spoken by fast-food restaurant employees who take your order in the drive-through lane.

SQUEEBIES
(skwee' beez)

n. The incessant nerve-wracking sound of a Styrofoam picnic chest rubbing against the back-seat of a car.

STOCKNOSTIC
(stok nos' tik)

adj. Describes a store clerk who makes a trip to the empty shelf to "see for himself" when you ask if there is more of a particular product in the storeroom.

SUBPARMA
(subb par' muh)

n. The second lid beneath the top lid on a bottle of Parmesan cheese.

SURVOIDS
(sur' voydz)

n. The irrational walking patterns one makes at the shopping mall to avoid a person approaching with a clipboard.

SWANGLE
(swan' gul)

n. The exhilarating point where the height of the swing seat causes the legs of the set to leave the ground.

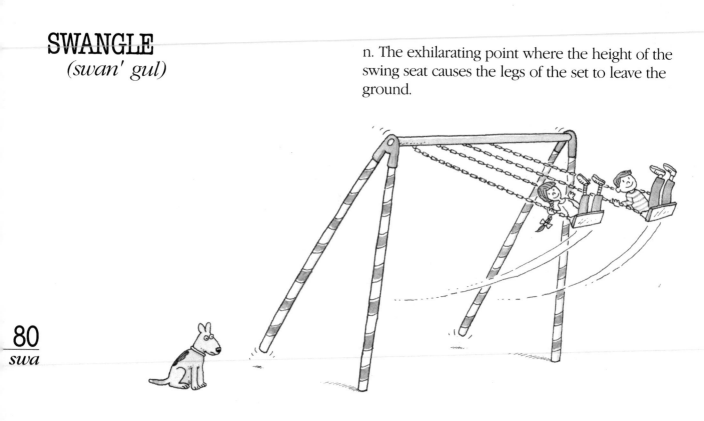

SWATUSI
(swah tu' see)

n. The little back-and-forth dance tennis players perform waiting for the serve.

SWEAT WORM
(swet' werm)

n. Any sweatpant drawstring that has retreated inside the waistband and must be "fished" out.

SYRAPORATE
(sir ap' or ayt)

v. The strange disappearance of syrup immediately after pouring it onto flapjacks.

TEARERIST
(tayr' ur ist)

n. The person at the movie theater whose only apparent function is to tear your ticket, leaving you with only half of what you once had.

TEMPTELLIGENCE
(temp tell' ih jens)

n. The ability a Thermos bottle has of figuring out whether something should be kept hot or cold.

TERRORNESIA
(ter or nee' zhuh)

n. The panic that occurs as you begin to introduce two people you know to one another and you suddenly forget one (or both) of their names.

TESTERNMENT
(tes turn' ment)

v. To bury one's paper in the middle of a stack to postpone the inevitable embarrassment.

THERMABUNIFEROUS
(thur muh bun if' ur us)

adj. The unexplainable property of your favorite chair feeling "hot" after someone else has been sitting in it, even though everyone's body temperature is supposedly the same.

THWOCK BISCUITS
(thwok bis' kets)

n. Biscuits initially prepared by thwocking the container against the edge of the counter.

TIBIAFIBULATE
(tih be uh fib' u layt)

v. When sporting a cast or visible injury, constantly having to recount the story of "how it happened" (thus leading one to bold "embellishments").

TIMEFOOLERY
(tym foo' lur ee)

v. Setting your watch ten to twenty minutes fast in an effort to be more punctual.

TOMIC DROP
(tom' ik drop)

n. "Factory testing" of a cat to assure oneself the "always lands on its feet" principle still holds true.

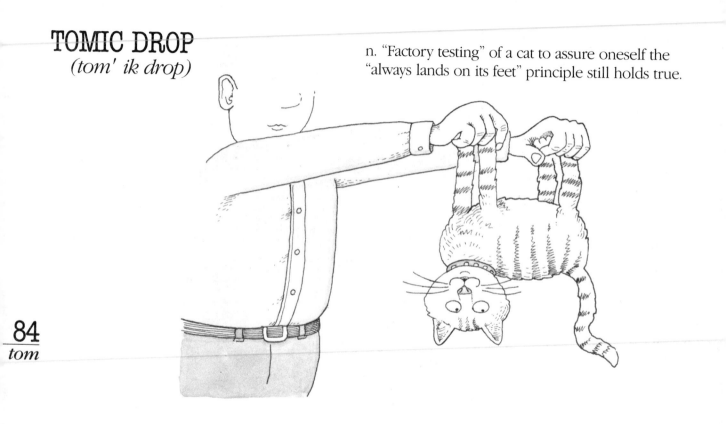

TRAFALSE
(truh fals')

n. Symbol used by unscrupulous students on true/false exams in hopes that the teacher is either very lenient or terribly nearsighted.

TRAFFILAPSE
(traf' ih laps)

n. The immeasurable amount of time between the moment the light changes and the jerk behind you starts blowing his horn.

TRIORITY
(try or' i tee)

n. Three things that need to be done first.

TUNAR
(too' nar)

n. Sonarlike device in cat food that, when opened, causes immediate materialization of cat(s).

TWIDCLIPPING
(twid' klip ing)

n. During the course of an office conversation, bending a perfectly good paper clip into a shape that is completely useless.

UBO (UNIDENTIFIED BAKING OBJECT)
(yew' bee oh)

n. The mysterious green stuff that appears in holiday fruitcakes all across America.

UNDERBERGER
(un dur bur' gur)

v. To lift the bun top and survey the interior of a hamburger before taking the first bite.

UNIPUKER
(yu' nih pew kur)

n. The hapless guy riding solo in a roller coaster. (See also **UPCHUCKEES**.)

UPCHUCKEES
(up chuk eez')

n. The couple directly behind the unipuker. (See also **UNIPUKER**.)

VERTEBRATRAMATRACIDE
(vur' teh brat ruh mat' ruh syd)

n. The fear of causing spinal damage to one's mom by accidentally stepping on a crack in the sidewalk.

WAMBLIE
(wahm' blee)

n. A pair of pliers that has been readjusted to the "crippled" mode.

NORMAL

CRIPPLED

WENDENSITY
(wen den' si tee)

n. The method of gauging an area's population by the number of visible fast-food outlets.

WISHAIR
(wish' air)

n. The deep breath you take just before you blow out the candles on your birthday cake.

91
wis

WISHUSCRIBBLE
(wish' u skrib ul)

n. Writing style one adopts when trying to stay within the designated spaces of a postcard.

WITLAG
(wit' lag)

n. The amount of time between delivery and comprehension of a joke.

WRANKLING
(rang' kling)

v. The unnerving habit mothers have of *gingerly* unwrapping and refolding the paper on a gift to save for later use.

WRIGLIMORTIS
(rig lee mor' tis)

n. The effect of a cold drink on a piece of chewing gum.

XIXELS
(ziks' ulz)

n. The lines above and below a string of Roman numerals that keep them from scattering all over the place (e.g., $\overline{\underline{XIXLVII}}$).

YARDSCHTICK
(yard' schtik)

n. Lame quips and rejoinders that neighbors have to exchange when they see each other in the backyard (i.e., "When you get finished with your yard, how about doing mine? Ha ha . . .," etc.).

ZERO POPTARTULATION
(zee row pop tar' tu lay shun)

n. The outer part of the pop-tart where no frosting or filling can be found, just tasteless crust.

ZILLA TRAPS
(zil' uh traps)

n. Those giant metal structures in which monsters in science fiction movies get their feet entangled.

OFFICIAL SNIGLETS ENTRY BLANK

Dear Rich:

Here's my sniglet, which is every bit as clever as any in this dictionary:

_____

_____

_____

_____

_____

Sincerely,

(name)   _____

(street address)   _____

(city, state, zip code) _____

SNIGLETS
P.O. Box 2350
Hollywood, CA 90078